Books by

MUNRO LEAF

THE WISHING POOL
SCIENCE CAN BE FUN
MANNERS CAN BE FUN
THREE PROMISES TO YOU
LUCKY YOU
READING CAN BE FUN
GEOGRAPHY CAN BE FUN
HISTORY CAN BE FUN
ARITHMETIC CAN BE FUN
HOW TO BEHAVE AND WHY
FLOCK OF WATCHBIRDS
LET'S DO BETTER
GORDON THE GOAT
HEALTH CAN BE FUN
JOHN HENRY DAVIS
FAIR PLAY
SAFETY CAN BE FUN
ROBERT FRANCIS WEATHERBEE
GRAMMAR CAN BE FUN

SAFETY CAN BE FUN

Words
and
Pictures
by

MUNRO LEAF

New, Revised Edition

J. B. LIPPINCOTT COMPANY

PHILADELPHIA   NEW YORK

Revised Edition

Library of Congress catalog card number 61-14579

Printed in the United States of America

Anyone who thinks
that being safe is
being a
sissy
doesn't know anything
at all.

If we don't take care
of our

heads

and our

necks

and our

arms

and our
bodies

and our
legs

4

we will have to stay
in hospital
beds
until
we
are
so

old we never

will

have

any

fun.

There are a lot of people who are always getting hurt one way or another.

Some of them can't help it, but some of them can. The ones who get hurt because they are

foolish

Are—

NIT-WITS

AND THIS BOOK

IS FULL OF

THEM

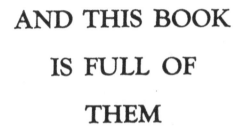

Here is a Nit-Wit who climbed into the shower and turned the hot water on before it turned the cold water. Now it can't start over again and do it the right way because it will get boiled red all over like a lobster.

What is just as bad as that is that it left the soap on the bottom of the tub and if it doesn't watch out it will slip and break something.

It is a Bath Room Nit-Wit.

This is a Downstairs Nit-Wit.

One thing it did wrong was to run downstairs but the worst thing it did was to leave its train on the steps. You can see that the train isn't going to be any good any more and I doubt if this Nit-Wit is either by the time it hits that bottom step.

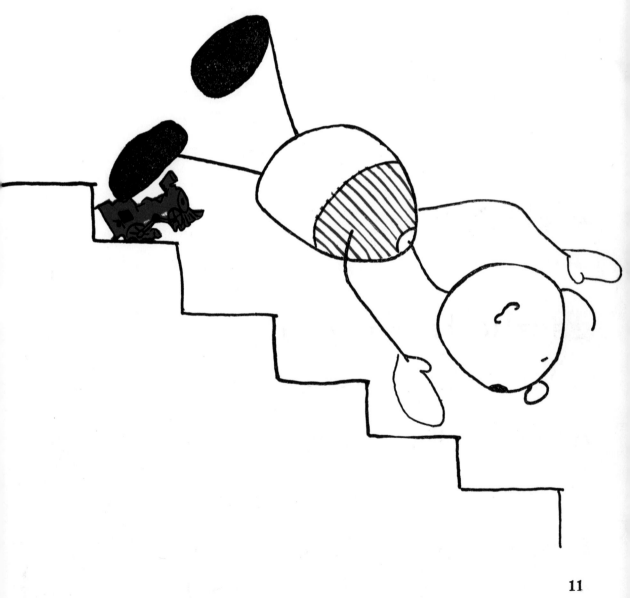

This is a Nip and Nibble Nit-Wit.
This foolish, foolish little thief goes
around the house hunting for things
to Nip out of bottles or Nibble out of
boxes.   It eats or drinks anything it
can find that looks pretty to it.

This one stole from the medicine
cabinet, the kitchen, the garage and
now it is taking its mother's nail
polish.   When it eats and drinks the
pills, powders, lighter fluid, soaps and
medicine it has piled up for a party—
it is going to be badly poisoned.

Too bad!

This one is a Never Look Nit-Wit.
It walks off curbs and into the
road without looking to the right or
left. It just walks along slowly with its
nose up in the air.

See that steam roller coming up the
road? Well, if this Nit-Wit doesn't
look pretty soon, it will be rolled as
flat as a pancake.

That scared thing you see behind all

that smoke is a **Fire-bug Nit-Wit**. It

just had a surprise and an awful shock

from playing with electrical wires.

It is such a baby that it doesn't

know that matches and fuses are not

to be played with. It thinks they are

toys.

MATCHES

Say goodbye to this No Brains - No Breath Nit-Wit. It is going to put that plastic bag over its head. Then it is going to crawl inside that old refrigerator and close the door so it can't get out.

Either one may keep it from breathing ever again — so say goodbye now — or tell it to stop doing such stupid things.

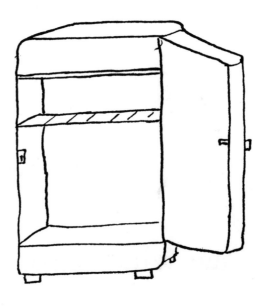

This is a very sad Nit-Wit and it has a good reason to be. It was crazy enough to run with a lollypop in its mouth.

When it fell down, any one can see what happened to the lollypop. At least we can see the stick still, but nobody knows whether they'll ever be able to pull the rest of it out. What a Stick-in-the-Mouth Nit-Wit!

This sad sight is an Animal Petting Nit-Wit. Most dogs are gentle enough, but there is no sense in sticking your hand out at strange ones.

This Nit-Wit did just that and now it looks as though it will have to stay there for the rest of the day and maybe all night, unless that dog gets hungry.

This is a Dare Dumb Nit-Wit. Just let anybody dare this silly creature to do anything and it will try.

Somebody said that he dared DARE DUMB to jump down these steps and he is just stupid enough to do it. He won't make it and will break his leg or head.

Dare Dumbs aren't brave — they are just goofy.

This will give you an idea of what happens to a Hanger-On Nit-Wit when it hangs on behind a truck and the truck really starts to go.

This is one scared Nit-Wit because it hasn't any idea of how it can let go now without landing with an awful thud.

Have a look before she hits the floor

with a thud.   This is a Bed Bouncer

Nit-Wit.

If all she breaks is the bed, she

will be lucky, but then she should be

punished and that won't be much fun.

There are better ways and safer

ways to have fun than to bounce on

beds.

This is a Water Nit-Wit that tried to

swim much too far when no one was

with it to help.

Unless that fish pulls it up to the

top, this Nit-Wit is going to be very

much too full of water.

This thing sitting here so bored and foolish looking is a Sharp Edge Nit-Wit. It stuck pens and pencils around its eyes so much that they had to put a screen on them.

Then it played with knives, razors, scissors and an axe until it had cut off the end of its necktie, chopped its shoe and taken a nick out of its ear. So they had to tie its hands up.

33

This is a Chair Tipper Nit-Wit. OH

BOY, OH BOY! is this Chair Tipper

going to get a bump when it lands

backwards.

How many times does it have to

hurt itself or the furniture before it

will learn to keep all four chair legs

on the floor where they belong?

This is a Wrong Door Nit-Wit. Here it is all tangled up in the bumper of a car that was passing by just as it stepped out of the door on the wrong side of the car it was in. If this automobile had been going faster this Nit-Wit would not still be all in one piece.

Here is somebody about to get into a lot of real and serious trouble. This is a Tool Foolish Nit-Wit.

You can see that it knows that it is doing something wrong. When that Machinery starts it is going to wish it had left the tools alone the way its father told it to. If that saw or chisel doesn't make little pieces of him, he may obey the next time.

By the time this one had touched a

hot stove and a hot radiator everybody

decided that they had better put its

hands in cakes of ice and tie a ther-

mometer around its neck.

Maybe that will teach this Hot

Hand Nit-Wit not to put its hands on

things that burn.

STOVE

Somewhere in the middle of all this

mess you will find a Bicycle Nit-Wit.

It rode down the wrong side of the

road carelessly, without looking out for

traffic and a car pushed it into a ditch.

Anyone so foolish shouldn't be

allowed on wheels of any size.

This silly show-off is a New Building Nit-Wit. It goes around looking for new buildings to climb on when the workmen have gone home.

It doesn't have sense enough to know that places like that are dangerous and are not meant to be playgrounds.

You had better take a quick look at this Explosion Nit-Wit, because any minute now it is likely to be blown right out of here.

Any simple minded person knows that guns and fireworks are not to be treated like toys but, this Nit-Wit doesn't. So it will be a race to see which blows him out first.

A Never Wait Nit-Wit doesn't wait

at corners for traffic lights or policemen

to say go. It just races out and tries

to get across before anything can hit it.

One car just missed the Nit-Wit

this time but I hate to think what will

happen when that truck it doesn't see

gets up to it.

This Nit-Wit is so stupid about walk-

ing on the wrong side of roads where

it can't see cars coming that its mother

had to do something to keep people

from hitting it. So she makes it walk

around with a danger flag on its head

as though it were a hole in the road.

It's a Dumb-walking Nit-Wit.

This is a Seat Standing Nit-Wit who was standing up on the back seat of an auto just before it went around a corner and came to a quick stop.

This Nit-Wit wouldn't think of standing up in a chair at home and after this it probably won't stand up in seats anywhere any more if they ever get it out of this mess.

This is probably all you will ever see of this one.

It is a Head-out-the-Window Nit-Wit and as you can see by its neck, it has its head out the window of this car right now. It may get it back in before another car or something else bumps it, but we doubt it.

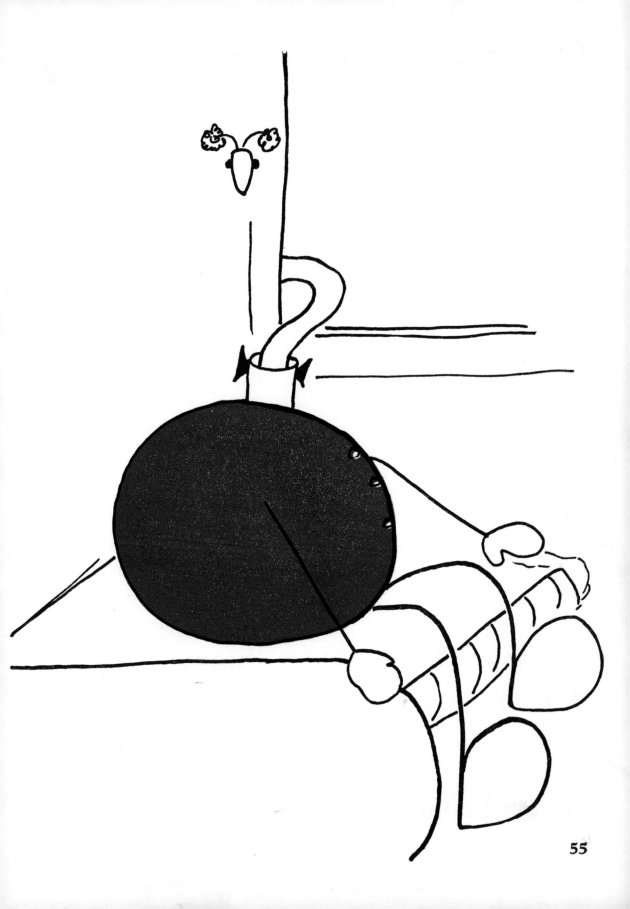

Careless Nit-Wits leave their skates and

balls around on the floor and some-

times other people fall on them, but

this time these two Nit-Wits slipped

and fell on their own things—

And Did they take bumps?

Here you see a Climbing Nit-Wit. It acts so much like a monkey, climbing all over the place, reaching up on shelves to get things it should not and spoiling all the furniture, that its mother is beginning to wonder if that little bump on its rear end is going to grow to be a real monkey tail.

59

This is a Selfish Nit-Wit. See that handkerchief with its initials on it? Well it never holds it up to its mouth and nose when it coughs and sneezes. It just lets other people catch its colds.

That S. N. W. might stand for Silly Nit-Wit too, because you can see it drinks water out of any old place at all—even fire buckets and old tin cups.

This is probably
the most stupid one of all.
It is an Automobile
Riding Nit-Wit who goes
along with people when
they drive faster
than they should.
What a Nit-Wit!

NOW WHY DON'T YOU MAKE

A BOOK ABOUT OTHER

NIT-WITS

THAT YOU KNOW

AND

SAY

THE

PICTURES

ARE

DRAWN

BY

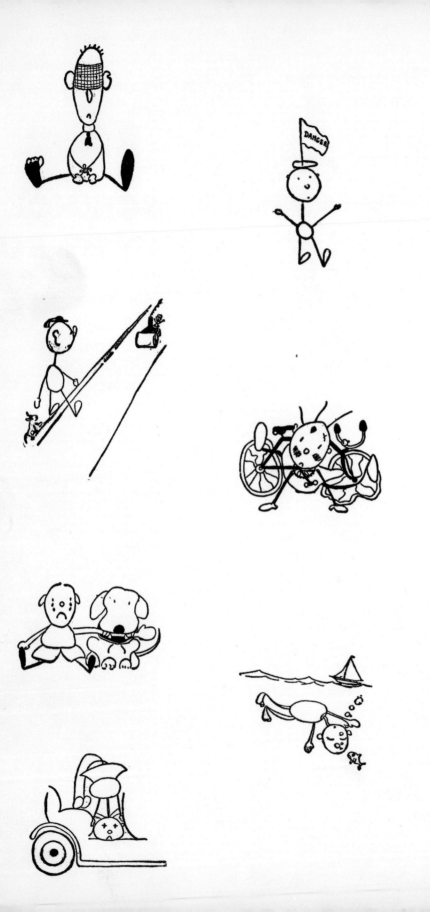